The Keeping

poems by

Linda Neal Reising

Finishing Line Press
Georgetown, Kentucky

The Keeping

Publisher: Leah Maines

Editor: Christen Kincaid

Cover Art and Design: Teresa Roy

Author Photo: Emma Carner, Emma Carner Photography

Order online: www.finishinglinepress.com
           also available on amazon.com

Author inquiries and mail orders:
Finishing Line Press
P. O. Box 1626
Georgetown, Kentucky 40324
U. S. A.

Table of Contents

*For Jim, who always believes
in me more than I believe in myself.*

*For my family by chance
and the First Mondays Writers,
my family by choice.*

Introduction

What strikes one first about *The Keeping* is Linda Neal Reising's proficiency at writing portrait poems with evocative details bringing character alive. It's like a short story writer putting together a sequential series that becomes a novel of place. Her images are so vibrant we believe her pen is a painter's brush. Her tributes to Mary Oliver, with its refrain of "I want to see with Mary's eyes," and to Jane Kenyon, in which she relates her work to the August paintings of Wyeth, show how much she learned from her models. Reising writes of family members, relatives, childhood friends, classmates, and local down-and-outs until you think she's exhausted the possibilities of the portrait poem. In "Like Wild Paints," about a fan bus trip to watch a baseball game against an Indian boarding school, she describes herself and her Oklahoma friends as "Cherokee, Shawnee / Wyandotte - but paler, bleached / by Irish or Scottish blood," unlike their rivals, "Seminoles freighted from Florida swamps / or Lakota hauled from the Black Hills."

Then, however, Reising surprises us with another section of equally vivid portraits: of animals, birds, insects, flowers, plants, with luminous detail. As in her portraits of humans, the vivid details make us see, with a rhythmical music that lingers in our ears, what she shows. In a late December poem, "Even the geese / late in leaving, / veer low, ringing out / so little time between dark and dark." In singing of nature, Reising's Native American heritage, Cherokee, comes through subtly. With a visionary combination of brilliant seeing and hearing, the poet recreates and celebrates, in the title of one excellent poem, a "Bounty" of life forms.

A later section presents a series of finely etched portraits, also animated by detail, of women of various ages and stages in life: girls, classmates, young women, mothers, daughters, grandmothers. Linda Neal Reising has the craft, discipline, and devotion to her subjects to bring a whole universe alive in this collection, surely long in the making. She sees the past in the present and all times as one. In speaking out of her Cherokee experience and heritage, but also the "paler" one claimed in "Like Wild Paints," Reising articulates a complex vision of the American experience and character. Her "keeping" of all that she sees and shares should inspire us to do the same. This book by an emerging major talent makes us yearn for more.

—Norbert Krapf
Indiana Poet Laureate (2008-2010)

Returning home reacquaints us
with family members and our former self.

—Kilroy J. Oldster
(Dead Toad Scrolls)

Our Mothers Would Not Let Us Watch

Our mothers would not let us watch
from any closer than the backyard.
There were no sirens
or flashing lights,
only a row of rusty pickups
and one sheriff's car.
The men were fishing the mine pits,
those gaping mouths that never swallowed,
except during July and August
when the sun glinted off the water,
sending a secret code to summer-bleached boys.
There was a fence,
but its sagging wires called sneakered feet to climb,
"Come learn the truth the parents try to hide."
They shed their clothes
and left them, shells on a chatpile beach.
The men plucked three bodies out
and gently laid them on the tailgates.
When my father returned,
I wanted to ask him what they looked like up close.
Were their eyes open?
Had the water leached the tan from their arms?
Instead, he grabbed my shoulders and shook me hard.
And his eyes were pools
that had no bottoms.

No. 7 and Other Heroes

My father went to school with Mickey Mantle,
A fact I once used to score points with men.
I wanted them to imagine my father,
Sixteen and sable-haired, winding up,
His biceps bulging like baseballs themselves,
Sailing a pitch across the plate,
Where The Mick waited,
All blondeness, buck-toothed and freckled,
Still shiny, before he drank away his liver—twice.
I hoped to paint an image of dark and light,
And just this once darkness triumphed.

> As the ball curves over the bag,
> Mickey twists his body,
> Forces the swing, too filled with his need to leave
> These chatpiles, to escape Oklahoma,
> To become *The Commerce Comet,*
> Blazing his way across sports page headlines.
> He waits for the smack of leather on wood,
> But hears, instead, Mr. Mustain, principal/ump,
> Yelling, "Strike three!"
> And for once, my father is the winner.

My father went to school with Mickey Mantle,
But he did not play baseball.
At nine, when Mantle was just learning to hit,
My father stood hunched over a cobbler's bench,
Like a dark elf in a children's book,
Hammering home nails into boot soles.
At twelve, when Mickey was playing catch
In a neighbor's backyard, my father was tossing
Freight into boxcars at the rail yard.
At fourteen, while the Mick was already practicing his autograph,
Dad hauled bricks in a wheelbarrow,
Watching as the mason sculpted the mortar
With flicking wrist, teaching my father his signature.

And while my father stood on an army base
In God-forsaken, Alabama, holding his breath
As a sergeant barked the names
Of those who would enter the arena in Korea,
Teams of young men who would sacrifice,
Whose names would be forgotten
Because they were not baseball heroes,
Number 7, exempt from one draft,
Pumped his "bad" leg around major league bases,
Came in sliding, and made it home safe.

Church Night

The first year Dorothy clutched
Toto's basket to her breast on primetime
and Scarecrow did splits in patched hand-me-downs
and Lion dabbed tears with his moth-eaten tail
and Tin Man spoke with his clipped metallic syllables,
I missed it.

Judy was already a lush,
wearing too-tight square-neck dresses
and resenting her doe-eyed daughter,
by the time the Wizard sailed his balloon
onto our brand new eleven-inch screen,
facade for mysterious tubes, lined up in back
like vials of poison in an apothecary shop.

All week my sister and I had waited,
my mother spinning tales of tornadoes,
flying monkeys, and melting malevolence.
But Sunday night was church night,
and there was no Glinda, sparkling
even in black and white, to rescue me,
to send me home with a click
of my patent leather dress shoes.

Hell-bent on heaven, my father
forced us all into his blue and white
Ford Fairlane and on to the First Baptist Church,
where Reverend Cosart ranted
against Kennedy, Papist for President.

Coming home, the storm began.
Living ten miles from the Kansas border,
I could believe that a house might be launched
like a Cold War rocket and set down again
on top of a witch or the Devil or Khrushchev,
while I huddled in the backseat, far away
from our cellar, built to double as a bomb shelter.

But that night, we dashed to the living room,
found filled with the odor of fire and brimstone.
Across the wall streaked a black finger,
pointing in accusation at the new Philco,
whose omniscient eye had been put out,
never exposing the false Wizard
hiding behind the darkened screen.

Johnny Keene

Waiting inside our blue and white Ford Galaxie,
my mother locked the doors just in time.
Down the street came Johnny Keene, cousin
to my father but rarely claimed. He lapped
one long leg in front of the other, like a squirrel
tight-roping a telephone wire. Talking to air,
he twisted his head, whirled as if fly-bitten,
before spotting us. Too slow with the crank
windows, we shrank away as he leaned
inside. *They're after me again.*
Before we could ask who,
F.B.I., C.I.A., Russians, he whispered.
How beautiful he looked just then,
his sleek hair ruffled crow-like,
his eyes so black and wide
they held a raven's wings.
No one's after you, Johnny Keene.
Confused, he pulled back,
walked away with rounded shoulders.
Inside the car, silence replaced the madness,
and the beauty.

Tornado Alley

"Tornado Alley" is what weathermen
nicknamed the strip of land I once called home.
In Oklahoma, early spring was when
the rivers rose from their beds, leaving foam
and driftwood along their shores. They called
the clouds to share a drink, go for a spin.
Then Dad would yell, *It's time to go!* Winds squalled
through cedars, bent double. Within the din
we ran, our heads turned down, pelted by rain.
The cellar door was propped open to air
the cave below: kerosene lamp, a stain-
covered mattress, a moldy quilt, one chair.
My dad would wave his hands. Bird shadows on
the wall flew south until the storm was gone.

Practice

(For My Father)

Lying on your back, mouth slack, you sleep,
while I practice your dying.
With practice, you told me,
everything becomes easy.

When I was a child,
you'd lie on your back in the summer lawn,
upraised arms veined and cabled.
The neighborhood children—
Vicki, Glenda, Muggins—
would line up, wait for your "Go!"
One by one, you'd send them cartwheeling,
elbows, grass-stained knees, dirty barefoot soles
tumbling, spoking through air.
I hung back,
going always to the end of the line
until you said, "Don't be afraid.
I won't let you fall."

I've forgotten the mechanics,
where our hands met,
how you managed the final push
that sent my world into revolution,
each time easier.

Now I watch you sleeping
and practice your dying,
hoping when it comes,
I'll be the one to say, "Go!
Don't be afraid."
Then take your hands and send you sailing.

Across the State Line

My father always picked up hitchhikers
if they wore uniforms or shouldered
their baggage inside olive drab canvas.
He'd pull to the side of the road,
tell my mother to turn the crank,
and a crew-cut head would poke through
the window with a *Yes, sir. Thank you, sir.*
The stranger would slide into the back,
duffle bag between his knees,
driving me closer to my long-legged sister,
scowling in the corner, daring me to touch.

The last one he picked up
was waiting outside Safeway, near the palomino
that would one day founder on dimes.
The G.I. looked older than the others—
pocked face, narrow eyes, nicotine-stained smile,
too eager. And though the cardboard read *St. Louis,*
we took him the two miles to Commerce,
told him *sorry,* and breathed a little easier
as he rattled our Galaxie with a slam.

A week later, a soldier hitchhiker—
this one baby-faced and believable—
kidnapped a family of five, forced the father
to drive to a played-out zinc mine
just across the state line,
shot them into the pit, took their Chevy,
and left so much to die.

The Spring

When Mr. Turk sold the farm—
Indian allotment lost to his family
in a card game generations before—
he made one last trip,
tottering to the east corner
of the front pasture.

This was what he would miss most.
Not the apricot tree,
heavy with miniature harvest moons.
Nor the three cedars,
Biblical in size, catching dust from the road
with their blue beads and feathers.
Not even the house,
whose parlor was haunted
by an upright piano, chipped keys
darkened by his late wife's fingertips
before the babies died,
before she sang lullabies
in Vinita State Hospital.

Bending, he hefted slabs of Oklahoma sandstone,
placed there to save errant hooves.
Beneath—the spring,
live water, bubbling, babbling,
with its sulphur breath.

People once wheeled their carriages
to this spot, filling their casks
with promises of healing and youth.
Even during those years
when the only clouds were dust,
only heat lightning cracked the sky,
the spring boiled cool in the heat.

One last time, he cupped his hands,
drank from the spring,
seeping up through rocks,
surging from its source treasured deep,
rising like an undying spirit,
reminding him that in the end,
all that lasts is stone and bone and water.

Rookie

In '53, when Uncle Jim was only fourteen,
his coach—the same one who prepped Mantle
for the Majors—drove him
to try-outs in his Studebaker Champion,
Perry Como crooning "Don't Let the Stars
Get in Your Eyes" on the radio,
while the two laced dreams like a pitcher's
mitt, waving pennants and hoisting trophies
all the way from Commerce to K.C.,
until they arrived at the field where felt-clad
Cardinals watched young men fly
around bases, send balls singing
over the fence, but when the pros
learned Jim's age, they shook his hand,
told him to come back in two years, not knowing
that by then, he would be a rookie husband,
staring through glass at the hospital,
watching his son, so small he would fit
inside a glove, struggling to win the fight,
while Jim, praying for each heave of the chest,
learned more than the coach could ever teach
about the meaning of a sacrifice.

Last Kiss

When J. Frank Wilson and the Cavaliers
headlined with Paul and Paula
at the Civic Center in '64,
on the same stage where Marty Robbins
and Faron Young in rhinestone suits
had once strummed their Gibsons,
twanged their country ballads,
I was there—having just sacrificed
my braids to an Annette Funicello do
that would never stay curled—
tagging behind my sister and aunt,
only a few years older but worldly—
sporting white pedal pushers, pocketed Chesterfields—
and even when Paula, claiming illness,
was replaced by a drummer in drag,
I didn't care since I was there for J. Frank
with his lacquered curls and inky eyes,
eyes that could not see on that summer night
the car wreck that would almost kill him,
the eight marriages that waited
to fail, his alcoholic death at forty-nine,
that title of *One Hit Wonder*, haunting
him to the grave, and as he grasped
the microphone and whined out *Last Kiss*,
I stood, swayed to the beat,
both of us on our way.

Benny

In sixth grade, we were voted
Carnival King and Queen—he
in his white dinner jacket, splashed
with a red carnation, posing
beside me, tiara-clad and sporting
powder blue satin skirt, overlaid
with netting, my short white glove linking
us forever on film.

In eleventh grade, I was voted
Most Studious. Benny ascended to *Most Athletic*,
and everyone chose to believe his bruises
came from team tackles, the black eyes
from basketball brawls, until the night
he put a gun to the chest of his ex-Marine
father, one red carnation blooming
where his heart should have been.

Like Wild Paints

Our fan bus shuttled past redbuds
and daffodils rambling foothills
as we neared the state line,
headed for the Seneca Indian School—
tall, glowering building guarding
the baseball field—where their boys,
year-round boarders, warmed up,
skin gleaming like copper kettles in sunlight.

We were Indian, too—Cherokee, Shawnee,
Wyandotte—but paler, bleached
by Irish or Scottish blood, not like these boys—
Seminoles freighted from Florida swamps
or Lakota hauled from the Black Hills and set here.

They never spoke to us girls—giggling and flirting
on the rickety bleachers—or even smiled,
eyes always averted, downcast, except
when they stepped up to bat.
Then they held their chins high—
warriors or gods or both—watched
as the ball hurled toward the plate,
then sent it orbiting into brambles
beyond the fence, before galloping
the bases like wild Paints,
their manes whipping behind,
with one thought—to run,
run!

Cruising Rt. 66, Miami, OK

(If I leave here tomorrow, would you still remember me?
—from "Free Bird" by Lynyrd Skynyrd)

On Saturday nights we'd cruise down Main
in the '52 Chevy my father bought
from a man who stopped driving at ninety.
We called it *The Gray Greaser*, giggled
at its old-person must and push-button starter,
and pumped it full of gasoline, one dollar at a time.

We'd roll into town before dark,
over the Neosho bridge,
past Ken's Bar-B-Que,
through Doc's parking lot,
by the Coleman Theater
where Will Rogers once twirled a rope,
around E.C.'s Drive-In,
and back to Doc's.

We were *faroutgroovyheavyman*
in our fringed suede jackets, fringed ponchos,
fringed boots—always on the fringe—
belting out Janis Joplin
from the rolled-down windows,
asking the Lord to buy us a Mercedes Benz.

Our faces—painted with peace signs,
bleeding daisies, weeping hearts— were framed
by long sheets of ironed hair.
We were masters
of the over-the-shoulder toss.

Once parked, boys would lean in through the windows—
boys who would go to jail,
     who would go to war,
     would go too soon—
including one who got famous singing
about a sweet home in Alabama—
even though he came from Oklahoma—
like all the rest of us.

The Final Push

My daughter has asked me to be present
At the final push
When she brings to light her son,
This boy whose shadowy profile
And bird-like heart have already set us
Cooing like huddled doves.
This child will share my father's name,
A name he wished to give his own son
Fifty years ago, a dream displaced
By daughters.
But I do remember
The relief flickering across his face
When night after night the news
Played out in the living room,
Cast its glow across the blue and orange
Floral cushions and family photographs.
The cameras caught the faces of young men,
No older than my sister and I,
Jostled on gurneys through swamps
And fields of elephant grass,
Blown flat by the fanning of helicopter blades.
The soldiers looked beyond the lens.
Did they think of their mothers,
Those women who gave them life,
Who strained, vessels breaking,
To deliver them to this early death?
Or perhaps they thought of the seeds,
Left unsown inside them,
Their fathers' names blasted—
Shrapnel on the battlefield
As the sons made their final push.

Desperado

You better let somebody love you,
before it's too late.
—From "Desperado"
by the Eagles

Hard to believe—

        you who flew in from Vegas for a few weeks
        each school year and again every summer
        to stay with a grandmother, too gray
        and vague to care what you did,
        while your mother toured
        with her second husband, a star
        on the strip, not quite a member
        of the Rat Pack, but still a lounge singer,
        bow-tied and bronze on the *Dean Martin Show*,
        crooning about a band of gold
        although he'd marry four times.

Hard to believe you died—

        you, who in fifth grade,
        wore a Fab Four wig and white turtleneck
        to school—looking just like Paul,
        the cute Beatle, while we girls
        lined up to have our pictures snapped
        with you, ice cube flash ratcheting
        atop the black box, while the Oklahoma
        boys, dressed in their Western shirts
        with pearl snaps, scowled
        just outside the frame.

Hard to believe you died in a nursing home—

        when I can still see you at the junior high dance,
        where the other boys lined the walls
        of the V.F.W. like targets in a carnival game,
        while you put on a 45 of James Brown's
        "I Feel Good," and in your metallic blue
        shirt, silken sleeves flapping
        against your mock microphone, slid
        across the floor—smooth with years
        of shuffle—lip-synched, twirled,
        went to your knees, silently squealing
        in all the right places.

Hard to believe you died in a nursing home—alone—

        you, who brought your guitar
        to high school French class,
        got away with correcting the teacher
        because you had been to *the* Paris,
        not the one in Texas, then convinced her
        to let you play, gathering us 'round
        as you strummed old Pete Seeger tunes,
        then, closing your eyes, belted a rendition
        of "Desperado," too young to know
        the song's ending was also meant for you.

Re-Writing Family History

Let's say you do meet
at the candy counter of Woolworth's
Five & Dime as she counts back mills
from your pack of Juicy Fruit purchase.

And let's say you do ask her out,
and she agrees to a movie at the Coleman,
afterward a burger at Doc's Tarry Awhile.

But let's say this time you don't elope
after eleven months, motoring
across the Arkansas line to stand
before the J.P.—she vestal
in her white graduation dress,
and you, sweating in your borrowed suit.

Let's say instead that she gives in
and takes you to her room
above the First National—the only place
she's ever lived on her own.

We can see her, shy—shaking with doubt
or desire—fumbling with her blouse,
and you gently helping
with each cloth-covered button.

Let's say you lead her to the Murphy bed,
tell her she's more beautiful than Rita Hayworth.
and once you are spent, we see you leave
while she sleeps, her black curls
splaying across the white pillow case.

Let's say this time you stay in school, escape
the draft. Your clean nails clack on the typewriter
as you finish your thesis on Stand Watie,
Cherokee general, last to surrender.

And there you are lecturing to rooms
filled with chalk dust and young women
who pass notes to each other about passes
they wish you'd make.

While she goes back to the candy counter,
waiting for your return,
plopping scoops of gumdrops onto the silver scale,
weighing her options.

Nature is the source of all true knowledge.

—Leonardo da Vinci

Every Little Being

I watch the angler drag the spoonbill
onto the riverbank, its side
bleeding from being snagged.
After the fisherman removes the barb,
the paddle-nosed creature
begins swimming through grass,
desperate to re-claim the Neosho.
It arches its back, lifts
its great head—gasping, gasping.

I'm reminded of something
the vet, hired by the county,
once told me—
There is such a will to live in all of us.

When animals were not adopted,
it was his job to euthanize—beautiful word
for *kill.* He saw it in every little being—
this struggle against death.

And then his wife, battling
for years, shriveled by treatments,
still strove to stay, even when he
told her it was okay to go. Still though,

he was haunted by the dogs—
their tails thumping against the table,
their gentle whines—the ones
who begged for their lives and, knowing,
still licked his hands.

A Place He Knows

(To Renny Golden—Twenty Years after the War)

You tell us you did not sleep last night.
The memory of the rabbit was too vivid.
You tell how you found him in the street.
His back leg, the one on the left,
hung limp, nearly severed.
The cars behind you honked
and sped around as you tried
to protect him under a plastic milk crate.

Finally, a young man stopped to help,
trapping the rabbit beneath the box.
Terrified, it beat itself against the latticed roof.
When you could not stand the thumping
and shrill cries any longer,
you freed him.
He limped to the grass just beyond the sidewalk
and stretched out his body, long,
all whispery fur and heartbeat.

You begged the boy to go for help,
to call the shelter, for anyone
who would value such a small, wild life.
He returned minutes later to tell you
what the woman had said,
to scare the rabbit back into the street
and crush it with the car.
It would be an act of kindness.

You looked at the rabbit,
its nose twitching against the grass,
and you could not be a part of it.
Eight years in El Salvador taught you the lessons of dying.
Let him smell the earth and feel the shade, you begged.
Let him die in a place he knows.

Redemption

At sunrise, geese begin sorrowing south.
The fields lie fallow, sporting brittle stalks
and flannel voles that scurry, look up, doubt
that life is long for them. Above, the hawks
leer down from leafless perches, flexing claws—
anticipation. Cattails and thistle
have released their breath. Remnants of wheat straws,
untamed oboe reeds, have lost their whistle.
This world is caught between—purgatory
of seasons. Even honeysuckle vines,
now scarlet, recall their days of glory,
regret the fences left unclimbed. No signs
of joy—until, confused by sun and cold,
a forsythia bush rings bells of gold.

Coyotes

(Thoughts of War on a Cold Night)

The coyotes mourn each night
for their moon-faced mother,
who waxed the sky
until it sparkled, then disappeared.

Or perhaps they grieve
for their children.
A neighboring farmer brags
that he's found a den,
dug near a drainage ditch
in his field. It's always best
to kill the young first.

When I was a girl,
hunters swooped low
in their red and white planes,
giant hawks, chasing the coyotes
from their holds,
while pick-ups with howling
wooden boxes in their beds
raced down the dusty roads.

The men freed whining hounds
and, clutching their rifles,
ran behind, whooping
war cries.

Later, the victors drove past,
slowly now, with corpses
draped over the hoods
of their trucks, the tails
flapping in the wind
like fallen flags.

There Was a Murder in the Field

near our house this morning—
fifty or so crows wearing Goodwill
overcoats, begged frozen soil
for seeds. There is something sad
about crows, as if they know
they know too much.

Henry Ward Beecher once said
if men had wings and black feathers,
few would be as clever as crows.
Not only can they count to ten
and use tools, but they also conspire,
gossip in regional dialects,
hold grudges when wronged,
and never forget a face. No wonder
Odin used two crows as his worldly observers,
symbols of *thought* and *memory*.

But, like us, there is something crows
do not understand—the stilling of breath,
the finality that comes with death.
When a comrade dies, they congregate,
beat their wings, and cry out to heaven.
Anger and grief held on their bitter tongues.

Summary Cannot Last

(In Memory of Jane Kenyon)

Flies fight their way inside,
then sit on table tops,
too stuporous to lick their legs.
These winged oracles prophesy,
Summer cannot last. Cold comes.

Gold stalks the corn fields,
and clinging to catalpa bark
are cicada shells, backs slit,
souls escaped.
The impatiens wither from thirst, neglect.
Salvia, once red,
pales to pink.

Jane would celebrate
this end of August,
muted and languid as a Wyeth print—
drowsy wasps, shadowed ponds,
dusk the color of eggplant,
the season's last tomato—
heavy ruby set in yellow leaves—
hay stubble, crows, crickets.

Jane would understand
this unnamed pain that settles
like migratory monarchs,
signing their message in a crop of ironweed:
Love and loss are a set of matched wings.

Clock and Compass

Yesterday, the dried leaf of a tulip poplar
broke loose in a gust
to become a Monarch butterfly.

Just when I thought they weren't coming
this year, these voyagers have arrived.
Now, inhaling and exhaling their wings,
they breathe life into the corpses
of windfall apples rotting on the drive.

I've read that Monarchs need
only a clock and a compass
to find their way back each fall,
navigating over seas of cornfields,
green oceans of forest.

Their eyes are the clock,
ticking off the hours in watchful
waiting until their wings become sails,
skimming the waves of southern breezes.

Their compass is the sun,
guiding star these sailors follow,
drifting, glistening gold and onyx.

A compass, a clock.
Nothing more is needed
until they reach home port
and pull in their oars to rest.

So Little Time

Late December—
    So little time between dark and dark.

    The morning wears a caul
    that it cannot shed,
    an omen, seventh sense,
    warning of winter's grayness to come.

    A lone chrysanthemum,
    spilling its last gold against the brick wall,
    is the only sunshine
    likely to show its lion face.

    Stripped silver maples
    stand over the remains of their comrades—
    felled last fall but still lying,
    still and darkly decaying—

    while a murder of crows in their black suits
    pace like undertakers
    with their hands behind their backs,
    tilting their pomaded heads in mock sympathy.

    Even the geese,
    late in leaving,
    veer low, ringing out
    Fly? Why? Fly? Why?

    These days are measured by little tasks
    left undone, and now…
    so little time between dark and dark

Taking Leave

Off he went. Didn't even leave us a message.
　　　　　—Rob Yarrell from the National Aquarium of New Zealand,
　　　　　commenting on the escape of Inky, the octopus.

How long did he plot the escape,
etching upon aquarium glass Roman
numerals only he could see—one
tentacle touch for each day of the years
since a fisherman trapped him inside
a crayfish pot—counting every moon
cycle, tide swell, he missed. Inside
his cranium, he must have mulled
the possibility, his cephalopod brain
churning, forming a mental map,
waiting for one mistake, a gaffe, a gap
at the tank's top. And how his three
hearts must have beaten when at last
he saw his chance. Blue blood pulsing,
he contorted his way through, slid down
the side, a desert of concrete spread
before him. Limbs becoming legs,
he crossed to the drain pipe leading
into Hawke's Bay. And at that moment
of leaving, he knew what he must do—
draw inside himself, become so small,
lose the form he'd come to know
if he ever wished to once again
hold the sea's immensity in his arms.

Mary's Eyes

(To Mary Oliver)

I want to see with Mary's eyes:
how the cattails turn to ermine
then shed their white fur.

How the blackberries, nearly ripe,
hang from brambles like garnet earrings.

How mushrooms rise
from under the darkness of damp leaves,
sheltered by wide-brimmed sun hats.

I want to see with Mary's eyes:
legs of blue herons
scruffs of owls
crowns of crows.

I want to see the colors
of honey caught in comb
dragonflies
plum blossoms.

I want to see with Mary's eyes:
how Virginia creeper clings
to stone walls with fragile fingers.

How tree roots crawl above ground
like backs of submerged serpents.

I want to see with Mary's eyes:
Spider webs, seeds, snow.

The way lightning fragments darkness.
The way a doe waits, watches.

I want to see with Mary's eyes
all of nature's metaphors,
see them so clearly
I can let them go.

Bees

I

When our bees first arrived that summer,
 they hovered so high above ground,
at the eave of our house,
that they looked like mist, wavering aura,
a ghost abuzz with promise of rebirth,
creating a new colony forty feet high
in a space left by careless carpenters.
The local bee man came with his smoker,
pushed back his cap on his upturned head,
already shaking. *Too high.*
Judas-like, he slipped us another man's name—
hired killer—
swore us to secrecy.
In the aftermath,
I swept their remains from the porch,
hundreds of husks tumbled together.

This year the honeybees have disappeared,
not even leaving fragments
of transparent wings or velvet shawls,
dropped in ecstasy during tremble dances.
Nothing. An apian Jamestown
without cryptic words carved into comb.
Colonies simply gone.
One keeper proposes a theory—
Rapture—
all the honeybees,
transported body and soul,
leaving us humans behind
in our barren gardens.

Bounty

For years the fruit trees have stood
barren in the front yard
where carriages once reined
up to the sway-back step,
time-worn stone still waiting
for perfumed girls to emerge,
dressed in party finery,
lace petticoats billowing
like April blossoms.

It has been twenty Septembers
since these trees bore bushels
of vermillion apples,
giant valentines, strung on branches
like glossy ornaments.
Since that season,
there have been only twisted limbs,
an occasional windfall,
shriveled, mummy-like.

Until now.
Now, in their old age,
gnarled by time's disease,
they stoop with the weight
of their own bounty,
hear their bones crack,
break beneath this birthing,
dying from their own desire to live.

Catalpa

After seasons of warnings,
it was one gust that tore the catalpa,
not lightning licking its heat
and sulphur tongue along her bark.

Winter after winter I pointed out
the deepening fissures
and limbs that hung empty
like an amputee's sleeve.

But each spring, triumphant,
she scattered blossoms upon my bed
of four o'clocks as if to say,
What's time to me?

You could not see
that the green she wore was a tangle
of poison oak and Virginia creeper,
sprouting like post-mortem hair.

Today, the men who specialize
in severed limbs and mutilated trunks
work in tandem, one inside the jaws,
the other flexing the metal arm.

When the droning finally drains away,
the three of you stand in dust blood.
She was hollow inside!
one says, thumping the shell. Echo.

The question now,
what to do with the remains?
The men only take down, not away.

From the window, I dream
of a cello player
who takes wood as his lover,
cradling her within his long legs.
He wraps his fingers
around her neck and strokes her
with his bow until she cries out,
Chopin! Chopin! Chopin!

Crawdads

Just west of the barn—
        three storeys fallen in on themselves,
        maple saplings and Virginia creeper
        sprouting, splitting its stones—
a pond once lay.

A pond where men landed bass
as big as buckets or barrels or boats,
depending on the teller.

Drained now of all but legend,
its lone channel cuts through the field,
quenching willow whips and blackberry brambles.

Along its banks are the moundbuilders'
fireless volcanoes,
pebbled mud lava spilling down cones.

These builders have steam shovel hands
and eyes that grow on stems.

Landlocked, they await the tide's return,
the swimming backwards into time.

Spirit Dogs

Fifteen years after rescue,
Angus, our peke/poodle mix,
dust mops down the halls,
no longer capable of climbing
stairs. He wears a goatee grown
white, professor emeritus brows
above eyes cloudy with cataracts.
Deaf as plaster, he feels
for the echoes we drum
out on wooden floors. Lately,
he has begun barking at air,
front paws lifting as he warns
the circle of spirit dogs to stand down.

During my father's last hospital
stay, he told me his brother
Harley, more than four decades
beneath the ground, stood each night
at the end of his bed, still wearing
a diamond patterned bowling shirt,
never speaking, pipe clutched
in the corner of his mouth,
cloud of black cherry smoke
forming a halo around pomaded
curls, as he kept vigil,
stroking the deep dimple
fingerprinted into his chin.

If I get to choose,
I want the spirit dogs I have known
to lead me over—mutts,
mastiffs, lapdogs, collies—
all dashing ahead,
then running back to tug
at my sleeve, lick my hand,
all the way to the Gloryland.

*I long to speak out the intense inspiration
that comes to me from the lives of strong women.*

—Ruth Benedict

Women at Forty

(A Response to Donald Justice's "Men at Forty")

Women at forty
Learn to fling open
The doors to rooms they thought
They'd never enter.

Not stopping at thresholds,
They carry themselves over,
Becoming brides again,
Bound this time to their unbridling.

And deep in mirrors
They do not seek
The face of a girl
As she practices smearing
Her mother's lipstick.

Nor do they search
For the mother's profile.
They do not need
To be daughters or mothers any longer.
Something has been lifted
From them, something

That is like the daytime sound
Of owls' wings, startling,
Leaving the limbs of pine trees shaking.

Kate

At ninety, my aunt tells me
she has had one hard life.
Nothing turned out as she planned.

A husband—gone now—
who was always gone,
working the pipe line through Alaska
or off the Florida coast,
exotic places he promised she'd see
as soon as the hay was baled
   or the calves weened
   or the hogs culled—
then he'd send her a ticket,
and they'd kick up sand
or slide down snowbanks,
but he always showed up
on the stone porch, scratching
the ear of their shepherd mutt,
ready to be welcomed
after the farming was done.

And the one son
she managed to bear—
before the doctor removed
her hopes—
a strange child with his books and rocks,
owl pellets and hornets' nests.
Gone now, too.

All she has left— a swarm
of feral felines and one rooster,
hatched on the back of a La-Z-Boy,
who every morning raises his beak,
puffs his scarlet chest,
and lets her know another day
is about to begin—
like it or not.

Eve

I first heard about Eve at Hudson Creek Baptist
where a blonde, blue-eyed Jesus, illuminated
from above, hung over the glass baptismal tank,
flanked by red velvet curtains that opened
and closed with tasseled rope—immersion peep show.
In Sunday school, Mrs. Reynolds had us read,
round robin style, the Old Testament,
stories about Noah and Jonah and Job's
boils, but instead of moving toward redemption
inside those gilt-edged pages, thin as skin,
we would circle backward to Genesis,
back to the garden where Adam, disenchanted
with naming creatures of the earth,
sacrificed a rib for God to cobble
together a woman, helpmate, mother
of all women, who listened to the serpent's
lisp, plucked a plum or apple, some unnamed fruit,
from the wisdom tree. Once again, we girls,
too young to understand the pain of childbirth
cursed upon our kind but old enough to share
the shame of our bodies, naked or not,
sat and blushed, feeling the blame we would carry
out of the classroom, marked as surely as Cain
for the sin of being Eve's daughters.

Beets

My mother waltzed inside
the old washtub, the one
that stood on tall, feminine legs,
tapered to points as if wearing heels.

It filled the tiny yellow kitchen,
with its rick-rack trimmed curtains
and black cat clock, wagging
its tail and eyes.

She put the beets on to boil
inside a granite pot, dark
as a country sky, sprinkled
with white stars. Inside the tub
went cold water, pumped
fresh from the well.

When the beets grew tender,
she slid them into the cool bath,
and my sister and I, armed
with paring knives, sliced off
their green Mohawks, then gently
slipped their skins away,
revealing steaming hearts,
straight from *Snow White*.

And sometimes we didn't wait
for the pickling, the mixture
of vinegar and sugar and cinnamon
that burned our noses, but bit
right in, red oozing at the corners
of our lips, trailing down our chins,
as if we were creatures
doomed to live forever.

And for a moment,
it felt that way.

Driving Lessons

I.

The farmer planted in rows
Packards, DeSotos, Buicks—
every car he'd ever owned—
where they grew along
the barnyard fence into rusted
temples of honeysuckle, blackberry,
returning to the earth
from which they'd never come—
sanctuary for all manner
of those that nest and web—
wayward hens, black widows,
bull snakes, field rats.

In winter, when their grilles
grinned through the overgrowth,
his late-in-life daughters—too old
for playing house, too young
for their own—would tug
passed-down coats over
feed-sack dresses,
pry open doors,
and slide inside.

Forbidden to drive by their father,
they took turns steering,
doing the two-step on the pedals
as they headed for Nashville,
to the Opry, live from the Ryman
on Saturday night radio—
Nashville, where women
could smoke and swear,
swig liquor and sing
about other women's men.

II.

When the farmer died,
his wife, alone now, took to driving
his '57 Chevy—white
and Caribbean-dream turquoise—
the only car on the farm
that still started.

She practiced in the pasture
bouncing along over tracks
once left in mire, now sun-baked
and rigid as steel, as she fought the wheel
for control.

One morning, she braided her hair—
hair he had never allowed cut—
wrapped the ropes around her head,
slipped into rubber boots,
headed out to feed the cows.
She loaded the trunk
with mineral blocks
and gunnysacks of grain.

But the hogs were loose—
burrowed free under wire, boards—
and when she tried to herd
them back with the car,
the boar blocked her path,
bristled defiance against her bumper.

First came reverse,
then drive.
He was left heaving out
his last breath of male indignation
as she tottered back to the house
to call her sons,
sons who would always believe it
an accident.

Odyssey

After the wise one
has regained his crown,
I ask the class,
Which character would you like to be?
Most boys, veins pulsating thirteen,
shout *Odysseus!*
It's not his wily ways they admire
but his arms, sinew strong enough
to string the bow
and tune it through the row of ax handles.
One boy, solitary, chooses Polyphemus.
I can feel him grind the bones
of eighth grade football heroes.
The shy girls, trying to unravel childhood,
vote for Penelope.
Others, already alluring in possibility,
sound off *Circe, Calypso*, even a siren or two,
aware of their calling.
Then they ask who I'd be.
Argo.
After their laughter,
I do not explain
how wonderful to love deeply enough
to wait twenty years,
to die in his arms,
even after licking the hands
of a hundred unfaithful suitors.

Karate Lessons

Women learning karate
Kick higher than men.
Their white pant legs flap
Like linen cranes taking flight.

Women, clicking bare heels, bow
Backs lower, straighter
Than males in the class,
Who resent the bending.

Women learning karate
Follow forms as if ball gown clad,
As if they waltzed at a cotillion,
Hands flesh fans, parting the air.

Women learning karate
Struggle with one lesson, the yell,
The bringing forth from deep within
The primal panther scream.

It is the hardest lesson for women—
This finding voice.

Ana's Dance

Inside the Flying Saucer Coffee House—
Haight-Ashbury on the Ohio—
the hushing hiss of the cappuccino machine
competes with poets—women in tiered,
sweeping skirts, men in woven sandals—
60's survivors. Listeners lounge on sofas
covered with Moroccan-print throws
or perch at tables lit with jasmine candles,
while in the corner, Ana, no more
than six, her arms chubby and tanned
beneath the spaghetti straps of her sundress,
sits drawing pictures of marmalade houses
with rows of paned windows, no doors,
and trees laden with fuchsia-colored fruit,
too heavy to bear. But when someone begins
to tap a beat on the Djembe drum or strum
an old Prine or Joplin song, she leaps
to her bare feet and begins to dance, her curls
a swirl of darkest joy—spinning, spinning,
spinning—a manic clock winding herself
forward into the future, her hands sweeping
the air, propelling her toward this finale—
white room, white gown, white hunger
riding through her veins—but on this night,
she knows none of this, only the thrill
of centrifugal force, twirling, twirling,
realizing, too late, that the only way to stop
is to fall.

An Educated Woman Explains Why She Likes Bluegrass

Because a fiddle can cry honey
or shapeshift into the Wabash Cannonball,
chugging its arrival
or whistling through a crossing
in some by-passed Ozark town.

Because a banjo plunks
like hail on a tin roof,
covering a barn with weathered sides.
Or like drops, fat and dull,
plopping into a zinc bucket, set below
the eaves to catch rain water.

Because a guitar can speak
with a country accent,
hum about mockingbirds and murders,
long for girls with names
like Sally Goodin, Liza Jane, Sweet Fern.

Because a mandolin quivers,
a timid soul, fluttering
like the wings of a blackbird
trapped inside a stone chimney.

Because the voices lift so high
and lonesome they drift,
suspended like Blue Ridge fog
just before fading to sun.

Miss Audrey's Wedding Chapel and Monday Night Pickin' Parlor

On Monday nights at six forty-five,
Miss Audrey's Wedding Chapel shapeshifts
into *The Pickin' Parlor*. The parking lot
brims with dually pickup trucks,
Buick sedans, and minivans. Old men cradle
their cases—fiddle, guitar, mandolin—
while widow women parade their finery—
lacy blouses, dangling charm bracelets,
toeless slides with blinking wedges.
They sashay past gauzy swags,
fake white lilies, net-shrouded tables,
as they head toward the back room,
filled with folding chairs and anticipation.

First, a bluegrass combo serves up
a helping of *Little Liza Jane*
before the Granny Chicks, straight
from their weekly gig at the VFW.
fold and unfold their accordions, wheezing
a '50's Willie Nelson song, written long before
he wore braids. Next, the ladies sit rapt
as a silver-haired cowboy poet drawls
Dan McGrew, and few care that he stops
and starts, says he knew it by heart in the car,
winks, grins, begins again. But most of all,
the people come to find a partner,
to hold someone close one more time,
dancing to every song, snubbing sin
as they two-step *In the Sweet By and By.*

My Mother Discovers Quantum Mechanics

In quantum mechanics
nothing ever has to happen.
The particle need never decay.
There is nothing to force
a real occurrence. Only conscious
observation causes events.
If we do not look,
nothing ever happens.

Ergo, if my mother does not see
my father, struck white with lightning
pain as his spine dissolves to chalk,

if she does not study his face,
gaunt and lined with the gray
dust of disease,

if she refuses to note
the voice too weak for song,
the shuffling step, the shaking hands,

he will for eternity be perched
in his blue recliner, remote
upright in his fist,
as he naps through *Bonanza*
re-runs, never having to die at all.

The Things We Lose

Two years into widowhood,
my mother is grieved
by his clutter, trinkets clustered
inside a fake leather box
with tarnished crest on top,
and she wants us to divide
the lot or cast lots, no matter
how it's done, just vanish
the last of it—tiny pocket
knives with nicked blades,
a parade of Mickey Mouse
watches, faux ruby cuff links,
Bill Monroe memorial belt
buckle, gold-plated union pin,
and two wedding bands—
one from Uncle Harley's first marriage,
the wife he traded for a bar
maid named Dixie, ten years
his senior—the second found
on a Halloween fifty Octobers
past, blinking in the night street
under flashlight beam, my father
stooping, pinching it tight,
finger against thumb, proposing
we check tomorrow's personal ads,
already knowing that most
of the things we lose
can never again be found.

That Last Spring Break

That last Spring Break before the girls—
my daughter and her friends—graduated
to their lives, we tamped the mini-van
full of luggage and headed to Padre Island.

At rest areas, March snow still
lined the swept sidewalks,
but when we reached the hill country
of east Texas, irises unfurled
their feathery tongues and wisteria
wove through abandoned farmstead
fences. We shed our coats and cares,
singing old songs—*Going to the Chapel*
and *Sugar Shack.*

Once on the beach, we shifted
our thoughts to sand and sun,
lounging like sleek seals,
glistening with lotion and heat,
while all along the waterfront,
on every restaurant menu board
or telephone pole, hung photographs,
pictures of girls just like these,
dimpled, demure, with MISSING
underneath.

And as we sipped virgin
margaritas under striped awnings,
the lost girls lay in the desert
across the border, their eyes open
to the same romantic moon.

Homecoming

How awkward
to be standing at a salad bar
in the truck stop café
of a one-horse, Route 66 town,
where you grew up too fast
too many years ago to count,
and where you think no one's alive
who'll remember you,
and besides, you have half the hair
and twice the you,
and everyone who could move, did,
to Broken Arrow or Broken Bow,
ordinary places with John Wayne names,
and no one knows
about the poems you write,
the ones about him,
the wrongs he committed against you,
when you were too innocent to know
that *no* should have meant *no*,
but you had no phrase
for it back then, only silence
that you've kept until now
at this salad bar, coleslaw spoon
mid-air, and he is there,
asking how you are,
and you smile one more time,
and say *fine*, lower the spoon,
and fork a pickled beet,
lift it bleeding onto your plate.

Jazzercise at Afton High

Two years into teaching, the Home Ec
instructor enlisted me to help bring back life
to this Route 66 remnant, with its blank staring
store fronts and deco signs, disconnected
when the turnpike turned the town into an exit
that no one took. Together, we crafted culture
out of crepe paper—leis for luaus,
roses for little Italy table settings, streamers
on costumes of one-act characters.

But our claim to fame was jazzercise,
each Monday night for nine weeks.
We advertised with posters tacked
to bulletin boards in laundromats
and coffee cup cafes. The first night,
we sat at the gym doors, cash box
between us, as the women poured
inside, two dollars a pop, a fortune
for us making seven grand a year.

The women came, dressed in polyester
pants or knit pedal pushers, women
of all ages and shapes. Women
from cattle ranches, where they spent
their days wrangling dust,
from hard scrabble farms, where they scattered
grain for chickens and gathered chickpeas,
from sewing factories, putting pockets
on jeans they could never afford.

Clad in leotards and tights, we took the stage.
Below us, a nervous twitter as we walked
them through the steps, turned our backs
so they could shadow our movements,
their sneakers barking on the polished wood—
Side step, side step, right.
Side step, side step, left.

Lunge right. Lunge left.
Go to the floor! Kick! Kick!

But the hardest move to teach was the shimmy,
requiring the women to put aside shame
while they raised their arms like goddesses
invoking rain, relaxed shoulders, and shook
from side to side. And just when I thought
all was lost, we popped Donna Summer
into the jam box, and every woman
in that room was transformed, a disco queen,
ruling her own fate to the beat of "Hot Stuff."

Totality

Eighty-seven revolutions around the sun
have landed her here, tucked inside a webbed
lawn chair, heat radiating from the driveway,
her driveway, but so many miles away
from the red clay of home, the place
where once, when she was still in school,
the teacher helped them construct viewing
boxes in which they could see the eclipse
or rather its shadow as it crept through the pin hole,
and now, she thinks, life has become like that,
a reflection seen backwards through an ever smaller lens,
except today, as she leans her head back—a corona
of white hair framing her cardboard glasses—
sensing the anticipation as the world turns sepia
first and then the cricket blackness of totality,
lasting for only a few short minutes before a burst
of light so brilliant, so unexpected, she says
to herself, *Yes, that is the way it will be.*

The Keeping

I have heard there are those who hack away
at grief, shearing sorrow over a lover's grave,
but my grandmother was not one.

Widowed after fifty years of marriage
to a man who thought women had no need
for swimming or driving or schooling,

a man who took her to the hospital
after the home birth of their fifth child
only when the bleeding could not be quelled,

but then carried her back to the truck
when the doctor said she should bear no more
children, a man who let her lie in bed

for a year, too weak to stand, while daughters,
no older than nine or ten, played mother
to the younger ones, a man who crowed

when the next three babies were boys. No,
my grandmother never cut her hair, steel-colored
braids coiled into a crown. And sometimes,

on Sundays after tail lights turned toward
other homes, she would sit with me, unpin
her plaits, letting her hair tumble, fresh-turned

furrows down her back, the silver brush sparking
tiny lightning strikes, like flint against stone,
untangling the hair my grandfather demanded

she never cut. A man once told me that a woman
only cuts her hair when she has given up,
but he was wrong. Sometimes, it is in the keeping.

Acknowledgments

And Know This Place: Poetry of Indiana: "Crawdads"

Comstock Review: "Final Push"

Fruitflesh: Seeds of Inspiration for Women Who Write (HarperCollins): "Mary's Eyes"

Heroinchic: "There Was a Murder in the Field"; "My Mother Discovers Quantum Mechanics"

Literary Accents: "The Keeping"; "The Things We Lose"

Lost on Rt. 66: Tales of the Mother Road: "Homecoming"

Naugatuck River Review: "Beets"

Nimrod: "Last Kiss"

Open 24 Hours: "No. 7 & Other Heroes"; "Benny"; "Like Wild Paints"; "The Spring"; "Coyotes"; "Kate"

Posey Magazine: "So Little Time"; "Bees"

Re-Writing Family History (A chapbook from Finishing Line Press): "No. 7 & Other Heroes"; "Church Night"; "Our Mothers Would Not Let Us Watch"; "Last Kiss"; "Practice"; "Benny"; "Like Wild Paints"; "Final Push"; "Re-Writing Family History"; "The Spring"; "Cruising Rt. 66"; "Tornado Alley"; "Coyotes"; "Beets"; "Kate"; "Homecoming"; "Driving Lessons"

So It Goes: The Literary Journal of The Kurt Vonnegut Museum & Library: "Johnny Keene"

Storm Country: "Tornado Alley"

The Poeming Pigeon: "Rookie"

The Southern Indiana Review: "Our Mothers Would Not Let Us Watch"

(Previously published as "Fishers of Men")

Writer's Digest Anthology: "An Educated Woman Explains Why She Likes Bluegrass"; "Redemption"

Writer's Digest: "An Educated Woman Explains Why She Likes Bluegrass"

You Are Here: "Women at Forty"

A fiction and non-fiction writer, as well as a poet, **Linda Neal Reising** is a native of Oklahoma and a member of the Western Cherokee Nation. Linda holds an M.A. in Humanities from the University of Evansville. She retired after thirty-two years of teaching English. She also spent four years as a staff writer for *Posey Magazine*, an on-line publication.

Linda has been published in numerous journals, including *The Southern Indiana Review, The Comstock Review,* and *Nimrod.* Her work has also been included in a number of anthologies, including *And Know This Place: Poetry of Indiana* (Indiana Historical Society Press), *So It Goes* (The Kurt Vonnegut Museum and Library), and *Lost on Route 66: Tales from the Mother Road* (Gondwana Press). Reising's poetry also appeared in *Fruitflesh: Seeds of Inspiration for Women Who Write* (HarperCollins).

Linda was named the first place winner in the 2009 Judith Siegel Pearson Writing Award, a national competition for poetry concerning women. In 2012, she won first place in the Writer's Digest Poetry Competition, as well as honorable mention. Her first place poem appeared in *Writer's Digest,* and both poems were published in an anthology of winning works. Reising's chapbook, *Re-Writing Family History* (Finishing Line Press), was a finalist for the 2015 Oklahoma Book Award and winner of the 2015 Oklahoma Writers' Federation Poetry Book Prize. In 2018, the editors of *So It Goes: The Literary Journal of the Kurt Vonnegut Museum & Library* nominated her poem "Johnny Keene" for a Pushcart Prize.

The Keeping is Linda Neal Reising's first full-length collection. Her second book, *Stone Roses,* is forthcoming from Aldrich Press (Kelsay Books) in April of 2021.

CPSIA information can be obtained
at www.ICGtesting.com
Printed in the USA
BVHW082123240920
589599BV00007B/102

9 781646 622726